Editing: Jan Burgess

Design: Peter Luff
Keith Faulkner

Picture research: Michelle Masek

Photo credits: Heather Angel;
Aquila Photographics; Frank
Blackburn; David Hosking; Eric
Hosking; Natural History
Photographic Agency; Royal
Society for the Protection of Birds;
Spectrum Colour Library

First published in Great Britain in 1982 by
Macmillan Children's Books under the series title
Macmillan Countryside Books

This edition published in 1987 by
Treasure Press
59 Grosvenor Street
London W1

© Macmillan Publishers Limited 1982

ISBN 1 85051 179 9

Printed in Austria

Endpapers: Tawny owl in flight.

BIRDS

DAVID ELCOME

TREASURE PRESS

Contents

Masters of Flight	4	Birds of the City	24
Feathers	6	Farmland Birds	26
Camouflage	8	Hedgerow Birds	28
Bird Language	10	Woodland Birds	30
Nests and Nestlings	12	Mountain and Moorland Birds	32
Migration	14	Birds of Lakes	34
Bird Tracks and Signs	16	Birds of Rivers	36
Day-Flying Birds of Prey	18	Birds of Reed Beds	38
Night-Flying Birds of Prey	20	Estuary Birds	40
Garden Birds	22	Birds of Sea Cliffs	42
		Index	44

Masters of Flight

Birds are not the only creatures that can fly. But as birds are so much larger than insects, we think of them as the real masters of the air. Over the centuries, human beings have tried to fly by copying the flapping wings of birds. All the efforts of the early 'bird-men' were doomed to failure. This is because a person's body-weight, shape and structure are very different from a bird. A man could never fly simply by fixing wings to his arms and flapping hard!

So what is it about a bird's body that enables it to fly? To start with, a bird has a streamlined shape and lightweight skeleton. It also has huge chest muscles. These are attached to the breast-bone, and flap the wings. But perhaps the most important feature of all is the bird's covering of warm, strong but light feathers.

Primary wing feathers

Secondary wing feathers

Finger bones

Lower arm bone

Upper arm bone

Breast muscles

Wings are a bird's arms and hands. Unlike human arms, they have flight feathers attached. The feathers fixed to the arm bones help the bird to glide. Those attached to the finger bones are more pointed and propel the bird along.

Swans are large birds so they have to build up speed before they can take off. They run across the surface of the water, beating their wings strongly.

For a bird to stay airborne, air must flow over its wings at quite high speeds. Birds have various methods of gaining the speed they need to take off. Small birds, perched on a branch, just fall. They rely on the pull of gravity to build up speed. Other birds have powerful legs so they can jump into the air. Then, to land safely, birds use wing and tail feathers as air-brakes. Their legs flex to absorb the shock of landing.

Owls have large wings compared with their bodyweight. This helps them to hover and also to fly slowly, using only a few wing-beats. This is a great advantage when they are out

hunting. These three photographs show how a little owl lands or approaches its prey. On the right, the owl is starting the downstroke. The wing feathers are tightly closed. As the wings swing

A swallow's wings are long and pointed. They enable the bird to fly and turn rapidly. To land on its nest, however, the bird must lose speed. As it approaches the nest, it flies upwards, opening its wings and tail to act as brakes. It can lose any further speed by flapping its wings against the direction of flight. Finally it is able to grip the nest-side and it feeds its young in that position.

forwards, the owl's body becomes more upright (centre). This brings the feet into the correct position for the talons to grab the perch or prey (left). If hunting, it then flies away, its prey gripped firmly.

Gannets can land safely, even on windswept rocks. As the bird approaches, it makes fine adjustments to the angle of its wings and tail. It tilts its head down to see the landing area clearly. For extra brakes, the gannet spreads its webbed feet and holds them out in front. The legs will flex to absorb the shock of landing as the bird touches down on the ledge.

Feathers

A male pheasant in his courtship plumage is very eye-catching. The bright colours are important in attracting a mate. On the left, you can see one of these feathers under a microscope. Different types of feather grow on different parts of the bird. Flight feathers are attached to the wings and tail. Layers of contour feathers cover the body and the front of the wings. Beneath are the down feathers.

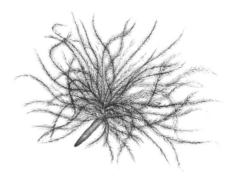

Down feathers are very fluffy. They trap a layer of air next to the bird's skin. This stops body-heat from escaping.

Birds are the only creatures that grow feathers. Feathers are remarkable in many ways. They enable the bird to fly. Overlapping layers of feathers give the bird a streamlined shape and also protect it from knocks and bumps. Feathers keep the bird warm by trapping a layer of air next to the skin. They also give birds their colour and pattern. This is particularly important for birds which are camouflaged to confuse their enemies. In some species, the bright colours of the male bird help to attract a mate.

Feathers are made of a horny substance called keratin. This is the same material which forms a bird's beak and claws, and human hair and nails. If you look carefully at a feather, you will see that it has a central shaft, with many vanes sprouting from either side. Under a microscope, it is possible to see that each vane is made up of hundreds of barbs. Each barb is joined to its neighbours by tiny barbules, fitted with minute hooks. These hooks interlock rather like the teeth of a zip fastener. If they become unhooked, the bird can link them together again by drawing the feather through its beak. This is what it does when it preens. A bird's feathers must remain in tip-top condition, and so it spends much of its life cleaning, preening and rearranging them. Sooner or later, however, they become worn out and must be replaced. When a bird moults, the old feather falls out and a new one grows to take its place. Moulting is a gradual process, for a bird would die if it were to lose all of its feathers at once.

The parent duck lines her nest with down feathers plucked from her own breast. This keeps the eggs warm. When they hatch, mallard ducklings are covered by a thick layer of soft down. This

Contour feathers are curved. They overlap to give a bird its smooth outline.

Flight feathers are a special type of contour feather. They have a stiff central shaft and stronger vanes than contour feathers. They are light but strong.

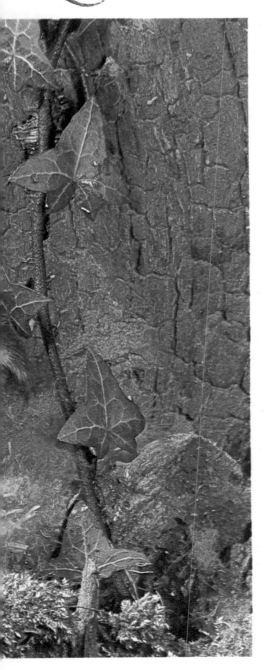

protects and keeps them warm during the first weeks. Ducklings leave the nest within hours.

The colours of feathers are due to the way they reflect just some of the colours present in daylight. The kingfisher's orange breast is created by pigments. The back and wings work rather like bicycle reflectors and give a metallic gleam as the bird moves.

Mallard duck spreads preen oil on its feathers

Wood pigeon water bathing

House sparrow dust bathing

Feathers must be kept in good order or the bird may die of cold or be unable to fly. Birds spend much time preening. A water-bird such as a mallard, keeps its feathers waterproofed by spreading oil over them. This oil is produced by the preen gland at the base of the tail. Most birds keep clean by bathing. They often flick drops of water through their feathers and afterwards dry themselves by wing-flapping and preening. In summer, house sparrows often make a shallow hollow in dry soil. They scatter the fine dust through their feathers. This dust bathing probably helps to get rid of grease and dirt as well as feather lice and other parasites.

Camouflage

Many birds are so well disguised that it is almost impossible to see them in their natural surroundings. This disguise is called camouflage. It is a very useful way for birds to hide from their enemies. The most common form of disguise is for a bird to match its background. For example, birds that live in snowy surroundings are often white. Snowy owls are concealed in this way. Ptarmigan change colour from season to season. In winter, they are snow-white. Later, they become mottled brown and grey to match the bare rocks of summer.

Robins and dunnocks spend much of their lives feeding among dead leaves. Their dull brown colours match the background perfectly. Female pheasants, grouse and many other ground-nesting birds also match their habitats. They complete their disguise by sitting very still and crouching low to avoid casting a tell-tale shadow on the ground.

Bands of contrasting colour can also conceal a bird. This is called disruptive camouflage. It breaks up the bird's outline, making it difficult to see. When the light falls on a bird from above, its back is well-lit, but shadows are cast on its lower body. Birds of the open heath or shore often have dark upper parts but are pale beneath to reverse this effect and confuse the enemy. This is called cryptic camouflage. In a few cases, birds actually look like another object which is common in their habitat. For example, the nightjar usually nests on the ground in heathland. As it sits on the ground, it looks uncannily like a fallen branch. This is a very effective camouflage which hides it from its enemies.

A ringed plover nests among the sand and shingle of a beach. With its contrasting bands of colour, the adult bird is hard to spot against its background. This is called disruptive camouflage. The eggs are also well disguised and look like the pebbles on the beach.

The red grouse is a game bird. It nests on the ground among heather, sedges and other moorland plants. The grouse would be a very tasty meal for a predator such as a fox or golden eagle. In fact, grouse are seldom taken owing to their excellent camouflage. Their red-brown plumage, barred with black, matches the background perfectly. When sitting on the nest, the female grouse remains without moving for long periods. She also crouches low to avoid casting a shadow. This means that eagles and falcons, flying overhead, find it difficult to pick her out from the

The plumage of the ringed plover chick is speckled and blends in with the general colour of the beach. When danger threatens, the chick flattens itself against the ground. This means that it does not cast a shadow which might reveal its presence to the enemy.

The common sandpiper nests along the banks of upland rivers and lochs. It usually spends the winter on the muddy shores of an estuary. The bird is brightly lit in such an open situation. The sun shines on its back and casts a

shadow underneath. The sandpiper overcomes this problem by 'counter-shading'. It has a dark-coloured back and white underparts. This makes it more difficult for a predator to spot among the mud and weeds.

background. Should all else fail, the female grouse has another trick to play. If a crow or fox came too close to the nest, she could lure them away by pretending to be injured.

The nightjar is a ground-nesting bird. It disguises itself by resembling some other object such as a dead bracken leaf or a fallen log covered with lichen. All day long, the nightjar sits motionless.

Even its eyes are kept tightly closed, or reduced to narrow slits, so that they do not show up. It is almost invisible. At dusk it flies off in search of food. It normally feeds on insects.

Bird Language

Like most animals, birds must communicate with each other if they are to feed and nest. Humans can put up fences and sign-posts to mark the boundaries of their territories. Birds cannot. Instead, they use a variety of calls, songs and visual signals.

Sound is one method used to attract a mate and establish a territory. Usually, it is the male bird which sings from a branch or some other prominent point. The message in the song is clearly understood by other birds of that species. To another male bird, the song means, 'Keep out! This territory is occupied and being defended!' However, to a female of the species, the song is an advertisement. The male bird is announcing that he is the owner of a territory and is looking for a mate.

Song is not the only kind of noise that birds use. For example, great and lesser spotted woodpeckers find a hollow branch and drum out their messages on it. Snipe, on the other hand, fly over their territories making frequent shallow dives. As they dive, they fan out two special tail feathers. These vibrate and make a sound like a bleating sheep.

Apart from song, other noises are used, perhaps to keep contact between members of a flock. Migrating geese, for example, often honk to each other to keep the skein together. Calls can also sound the alarm if danger such as a cat or bird of prey threatens.

Songs are particularly useful to birds that live in woodland, or other dense surroundings, where they cannot see each other very well. Birds of open country are more likely to use visual signals. They may have showy plumage, perhaps with bright-coloured wing bars or tail feathers. The showy feature can be 'shown off' to impress the opposite sex, or to threaten another bird. Usually this display is a sufficient warning. On rare occasions when it is not heeded, a fight may break out.

When danger threatens, some birds put on a special display, drawing attention away from the nest, eggs or chicks. One method is to feign injury. A lapwing may trail a wing across the ground as though it were broken. Once the fox or crow has been distracted and lured away from the nest, the lapwing makes a miraculous recovery, and flies safely away, leaving a confused hunter!

A few species, such as the black grouse, get together in groups or 'leks'. In the breeding season, the males, which are called blackcocks, gather together to show off their black-and-white tails and red head wattles. The birds parade up and down, threatening and fighting. The purpose of all this is to find out which birds are the strongest, and to impress the females. When a female, called a greyhen, walks through the lek, she is courted by each blackcock in turn. Finally she selects one of them. The males take no part in caring for the young.

Edge of territory

✕ Conflict area

● Song post

Robins defend their territories using song and visual displays. The robin chooses several song posts, and sings to let other robins know that it is defending a particular area. It will threaten any other robin that trespasses into its territory by showing off its orange breast, making loud 'tic-tac' noises, and flicking its tail and wings. A fight may even break out.

Some species of bird carry out 'courtship feeding'. With linnets and other finches, it takes place at the nest. The female begs for food from the male, just as the nestlings will later on. She flutters her wings, opens her bill and utters pleading calls. This probably strengthens the bond between the birds. It also prepares the adult birds for feeding the young later.

Nests and Nestlings

Many birds build nests as safe places in which to lay their eggs. A nest is usually a cup-shaped structure, built on the ground, among reeds, or in a shrub or tree. However, a woodpigeon makes a flimsy twig platform, while an osprey's eyrie may be a metre across and two metres high! Water birds such as grebes build floating platforms of dead reeds and water-weed. Ready-made holes are popular with some birds. Puffins, for example, lay their eggs in empty rabbit burrows. Blue tits line holes in trees with soft moss and feathers. Woodpeckers carve out their own holes and lay their eggs on a pile of wood chippings.

Some birds make no kind of nest. Penguins just balance an egg on their feet. Guillemots lay their pear-shaped eggs directly onto a bare ledge on a sea-cliff. The cuckoo is known as a brood parasite. It avoids all the effort of nest-building and feeding a family by laying its eggs in another bird's nest. Some birds, such as gannets, terns and rooks, form spectacular and noisy colonies when nesting. Other birds prefer to keep their neighbours at a distance. The robin fiercely defends the territory round its nest. This ensures a good food supply for the family.

Whatever the type of nest, the eggs have to be laid and incubated. The great advantage of egg-laying to a flying creature is that it avoids a long period of pregnancy. The mother bird does not have to carry round the extra weight of developing chicks. When the eggs hatch, the young cannot fly but they are reared in fairly safe surroundings. Young ducks and geese can feed themselves within hours of hatching. In many other species, the adults have to feed their young. Pigeons are unusual because the parents produce 'pigeon milk' in their crops, which they feed to the chicks when they are hungry.

Many young birds encourage their parents to feed them by begging. They gape, wave their brightly-coloured mouths and utter pleading calls. The more hungry the chicks, the more frenzied the begging.

The nest of a long-tailed tit is ball-shaped, and woven from spider's silk, moss and lichen. It is usually well hidden in a gorse

Blackbird

Great spotted woodpeckers hack out their own nest-holes with chisel-like bills. The finished nest is some 25 cms deep. In following seasons, it may be used by other hole-nesters, including starlings, nuthatches and tits. Woodpeckers feed their young largely on insects. The young woodpeckers scramble up to the entrance of the nest-hole to be fed. This one is calling for its food.

Blackbirds weave a cup-shaped nest in a creeper, shrub or on the ledge of a building. Birds know how to build by instinct, but they get better at it as they grow older and more experienced. It is usually the female blackbird which builds the nest. She uses grasses, leaves and mud, shaping the cup by twisting and pressing it with her legs and body. The hen incubates the eggs for about two weeks until they hatch. At first, the young get all their food from their parents. The lining of their mouth is bright pink and is displayed as they gape and plead for food. The young can fend for themselves when they are between three and four weeks old.

bush or among brambles. It may
contain as many as a dozen eggs.
The nest is flexible, so as the young
grow, it expands.

Arctic terns nest in noisy colonies
on rocky islands or sand-dunes.
The parents dive for small fish
which they carry back to the nest.

Tern chicks peck instinctively at
any long silvery shape, expecting
it to be food. This one is pecking at
the silver shape of a fish.

Jackdaw

House martin

Robin

Our own homes and gardens
provide many nest-sites. House
sparrows make untidy nests of
straw and feathers, usually in a
hole in the roof, or perhaps behind
a drainpipe or among creeper.
Jackdaws may build their nests of
sticks inside the chimney. House
martins make neat semi-circular
cups of mud pellets and saliva
which they fix under the eaves.
Sometimes, house sparrows take
over these nests. Robins and
wrens will build their nests in
thick hedges or bushes. They
might even find their way into a
garden shed where they will
choose an odd nest-site like an
empty paint-tin.

House sparrow

Wren

Migration

About half the birds of western Europe seldom move far from the place where they were hatched. Others, however, are among the greatest travellers on earth. By migrating, birds can escape from bad weather. They can also make the most of food supplies which vary from season to season. For example, the European swallow and cuckoo spend the summer breeding in Britain and western Europe. In winter, they fly south to the warmth of Africa.

The Arctic tern holds the record for long-distance travel. It breeds as far north as Greenland and Iceland. During the northern winter, it migrates south to take advantage of the southern hemisphere's summer. It feeds on tiny animals called krill, in the rich seas off Antarctica. Its annual round trip covers more than 35,000 kilometres. The journeys of other species may be shorter, perhaps simply moving from high to low ground in winter. Or they may move from an inland breeding-site to the coast.

☐ **Winter visitors to British Isles and Northern Europe**

■ **Summer visitors to British Isles and Northern Europe**

The British Isles are warmed by the waters of the North Atlantic Drift. For this reason, they are visited by many migrant birds. In summer, warblers and swallows come to breed. As they leave, wildfowl and others arrive from the north and east.

In autumn, house martins gather in large flocks on overhead wires and trees during the two or three weeks before they make the long journey to Africa. They are restless as they gather, waiting for the right weather in which to set off.

Scientists ring birds like this lesser whitethroat. It helps them find out more about bird journeys. The rings are made of aluminium. Each has its own number and address. If you find a ringed bird, do not remove the ring. Make a note of its number, where and when you saw it, and whether the bird was alive or dead. Send the information to the address given on the ring.

This willow warbler is being weighed with a spring balance. It is placed head-down in a polythene funnel so that it cannot harm itself. Some warblers put on a heavy layer of fat before migrating, greatly increasing their weight. It is used up as fuel on the journey.

Greylag geese are generally winter visitors to Britain. A few breed in the north of Scotland. Others have escaped from wildfowl collections and now breed in other parts of Britain. Those that arrive in autumn have travelled from their breeding grounds in Iceland. At this time of year, their food supplies of grasses, roots, and water weeds are hidden by ice and snow. Britain is an ideal wintering area, as pasture-land and crops are available for most of the year to feed the geese.

Bird Tracks and Signs

There is more to birdwatching than simply going out armed with binoculars and a field guide. There will be many times when birds are hard to see, perhaps due to poor weather or a dense type of habitat. Shy species fly off at the first sounds of a person approaching. On such occasions, it pays to be a detective. Look for clues left behind by birds, and learn how to interpret them.

Many birds are messy eaters, and food remains provide clues to identity. Look out for fragments of nut and cone, damaged fruit, or feathers ripped from a carcase. Droppings and pellets reveal the identity of some species. Also useful are pieces of eggshell, stolen by a crow or removed from the nest by the parent birds.

As birds are light, their footprints do not show up as well as mammals'. But look carefully for them in soft mud, sand or snow.

Owls swallow their prey whole. They digest their meal and then later bring up a pellet containing the indigestible remains. The long-eared owl above is ejecting such a pellet. You can dissect pellets in a dish of water. Try to identify the skulls and bones they contain. This will tell you a good deal about the owl's diet. There may be some insect remains. Other birds also produce pellets.

If you want to take up bird-watching, it is a good idea to equip yourself with a notebook, pencil and a good field guide to help you identify the birds you see. It is important to wear warm, waterproof clothing and boots. They should be drab in colour to help conceal you from the birds.

Binoculars are also very useful, and it is worth paying as much as you can for these. Cheap binoculars can distort colours and shapes, and are easily damaged. A magnification of 8× or 10× is ideal. Bird clubs often organize outings and provide magazines which will tell you about activities.

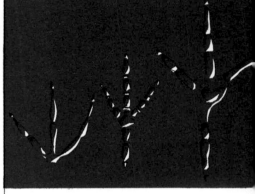

To make plaster casts of foot-prints, choose the clearest print you can find in mud or sand. (You cannot make casts of prints in snow.)
1. Remove any loose mud or leaves. Place a piece of card round it and push the bottom edge well into the mud. Pour in wet plaster of Paris and leave it to set.
2. When the cast is dry, remove it and clean off any mud. At home, place a wider piece of card round the cast, and rub a thin film of vaseline or washing-up liquid over it.
3. Pour more plaster of Paris into the mould.
4. When this has set hard, remove it from the mould. You can now paint the footprint. Remember to label it with the species and the place and date you found it.

reat spotted woodpeckers
ave clues to their activities.
hey often wedge hazelnuts or
ine-cones into cracks and
evices in trees. Then, the
oodpecker will chisel into the
ut or cone to extract the kernel or
ed. A heap of empty shells and
attered cones may build up
elow a well-used 'woodpecker
orkshop' as it is called.

Key
1. A tawny owl may mark its perch with white droppings, and will drop pellets to the ground.
2. A great spotted woodpecker uses its workshop to extract seeds from cones.
3. A sparrowhawk will often pluck its prey standing on an old tree-stump.
4. Jays bury acorns as a store for the winter.
5. A song thrush breaks snails open on an anvil such as a sharp stone.
6. Parent birds remove broken eggshells from their nests.

Of course, it is illegal to take the eggs of wild birds. Heavy fines can be imposed for egg-stealing or even disturbing the adults of some species at the nest. Too many birds have suffered as a result of people interfering with them.

However, it is possible to make a collection of moulted feathers which you can mount on card. Always store them with a few mothballs to discourage moths. It is also illegal to take or destroy birds' nests while they are in use. But in autumn, disused nests may be collected from hedgerows. Store them in a shoe-box with mothballs. Remember to label all specimens carefully.

Day-Flying Birds of Prey

The birds of prey are divided into two groups, depending on whether they hunt by day or night. Owls are mainly night hunters. Falcons, hawks, harriers, kites, eagles, buzzards and ospreys need daylight. Each of these day-flying predators uses a different technique to catch food. Falcons have pointed wings and rely on their great speed to kill prey. Most hawks live in wooded country and surprise their victims by flying, half-hidden among the trees before they pounce. Harriers live in more open country such as moors and marshes. They search for prey by flying to and fro, low over the ground. Eagles and buzzards soar on huge, rounded wings. They scan the ground below for food.

All birds of prey have powerful feet and talons. They rip the flesh into shreds with their hooked beaks. Their eyes are set at the front of their heads, instead of at the sides. This means that they can judge distances accurately. This is vital for catching fast-moving prey.

The peregrine falcon may reach speeds of 200 kph as it dives headlong onto its prey. It strikes with razor-sharp talons and kills its prey instantly.

When it has caught a fish, the osprey carries it back to its eyrie. The osprey's toes have tiny spines. They help the bird to keep a firm hold on its slippery prey.

The numbers of birds of prey depend on the prey available. In the far north, the lemming, a small rodent, is the main food of birds such as the rough-legged buzzard or snowy owl. The lemming population goes up and down, reaching a peak every third or fourth year. Because there is more food available then, birds of prey succeed in raising their young, and their numbers also increase.

The merlin is a small but handsome falcon. It nests on the ground on heather-covered moorland. It feeds mainly on sma birds such as meadow pipits which it catches in flight. The

The buzzard often soars in wide circles, up to a hundred metres above the ground, as it searches for food. It scans the land below with sharp eyes. Sometimes it uses a different technique. It perches on a branch or telegraph pole and when it spots a rabbit or small animal, it glides down to take it. It rips the carcase with sharp talons and tears off pieces with its hooked bill.

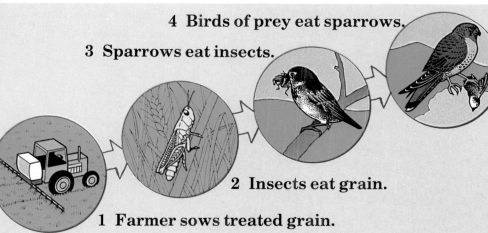

4 Birds of prey eat sparrows.

3 Sparrows eat insects.

2 Insects eat grain.

1 Farmer sows treated grain.

Predators are at the end of a food-chain. They live on smaller birds which, in turn, eat insects and seeds. In the 1960s, the numbers of birds of prey fell. Research showed that this was due to pesticide poisoning.

Farmers sprayed their fields with pesticides. The chemicals were then absorbed into the bodies of small birds. When these birds were eaten by predators, the poison levels built up. Many birds of prey were killed as a result.

The female usually lays four eggs, but it is the male bird that feeds the young.

Kestrels hunt in a different way from other falcons. They often hover, hardly moving at all, as they scan the ground below. In recent years, kestrels have discovered that motorway verges make good hunting grounds. They are untreated by pesticides so they shelter many small mammals and insects. You will also see kestrels in towns. They nest on tall buildings, which are really quite similar to the cliff ledges of their natural habitat.

19

Night-Flying Birds of Prey

Owls are the night-hunters of the bird world. Although they cannot see in total darkness, their night-time vision is better than most other birds. It is certainly far better than our own. The owl's eyes are very large in order to gather as much light as possible. They also have thick lenses which focus light onto the retina at the back of the eye. The owl's retina has a very large number of light-sensitive elements, called rods. This further improves its night sight.

Like other birds of prey, the owl's eyes face forwards, giving stereoscopic vision. This means that it can judge distances very accurately. Because so much of an owl's skull is taken up by its eyes, there is little room left for many muscles to control them. Eye movement is, therefore, very limited. To overcome this problem, owls have very flexible necks. Many can twist their heads through more than 180 degrees when they are perched. The owl's bill is hooked, although it swallows most of its prey whole. Some time after the meal, a pellet of the bones, fur and feathers is coughed up. Owls have large sharp talons. They can get a good grip on their prey because two toes point forwards, and two point to the rear. This means that, however much the prey wriggles, it cannot escape.

Owls probably rely as much on their hearing as on their vision when hunting on dark nights. They have unusually large ear-drums and openings at the sides of their heads, and fly silently. They find small mammals by listening for squeaks and rustles in the grass. Mice, voles, shrews and rats form the major part of the diet of larger owls. Bats, frogs, small birds and even earthworms are taken as well. Little owls also eat caterpillars and beetles.

Not all owls hunt at night. Short-eared owls do most of their hunting during the hours of daylight. Barn and little owls will sometimes hunt by day in poor weather.

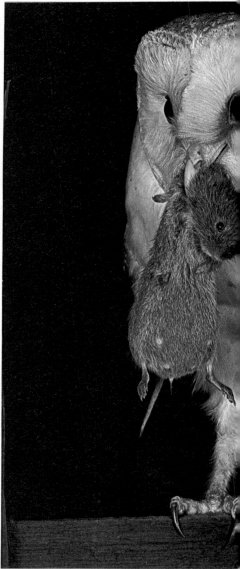

Sensitive ears can locate small animals even on the darkest night.

Little owls nest and roost in holes in trees, and are often seen sitting in the entrance in daytime. Although smaller than most other owls, they can still catch mice, voles and small birds. They also like worms, caterpillars and large insects such as moths, as you can see here. Little owls came to Britain in the 19th century and are now widespread throughout England and Wales.

Above: As its name suggests, the barn owl is closely linked with people. It nests and roosts in barns, church towers and old buildings. It helps control rats, mice and other pests.

Barn owls lay between four and seven eggs. They hatch at intervals of a few days. The young are fed on small animals caught by the parents. They hatch at different times and there is quite a difference in size between the oldest and youngest owlet. The largest one may even eat the smaller ones if hunting is poor!

Wings are muffled by velvet-like pile for silent flight.

Eyes face forwards for stereoscopic vision – good judgement of distances.

Eyes are large to give good vision in poor light.

Feet have sharp talons and a reversible fourth toe to kill and grip prey firmly.

The tawny is Britain's most common owl. It is even found in towns if there are large trees about. It is not found in Ireland, however. The tawny hunts exclusively by night and is well equipped for the task. It spends most of the day roosting in trees or holes.

Garden Birds

Most gardens are a mixture of lawns and flower-beds, shrubs and trees. To most birds they must seem just like open woodland. Indeed, many garden birds are also found in woodland areas.

The basic needs of any bird are food, water, shelter and somewhere to build a nest. Gardens can provide most of these needs for woodland birds, so long as they are not too disturbed. Blackbirds, thrushes and starlings find grubs and worms on lawns and flower-beds, and take berries from shrubs in autumn. Dunnocks, robins and wrens search for insects under shrubs. Blue and great tits find greenfly and caterpillars on trees, roses and other shrubs. They also eat seeds in autumn. Finches and sparrows are seed-eaters too.

You can make your garden more attractive to birds by giving them food in winter. They need water all the year round. If possible, allow flowers to go to seed and plant berry-bearing shrubs. Try putting a nest box in a sheltered spot. If you are lucky, your garden may even attract a woodpecker!

Some of the birds that visit gardens are shown in this scene. The birds soon get used to the presence of humans, but cats are always a danger. Bird tables should always be placed away from any cover in which a cat might lurk.

Nest boxes are often used by hole-nesting birds. You may need help with the more difficult bits!
You will need:
a piece of wood 150 × 15 × 1 cms; a piece of old inner tube or leather; some tacks; 2 hooks and eyes; 24 nails 3.5 cms long; a saw; a brace and bit (bit diameter 28 mms).
1. Cut the wood as in the plan.
2. Using the brace and bit, make a hole in the front.
3. Nail the back to the sides.
4. Nail the front to the sides.
5. Nail on the base.
6. Bevel the edges of the front and roof.
7. Attach the roof to the back by tacking a hinge of inner tube to each.
8. Fit hooks and eyes to fasten roof.
9. Fasten to a tree or wall facing north.

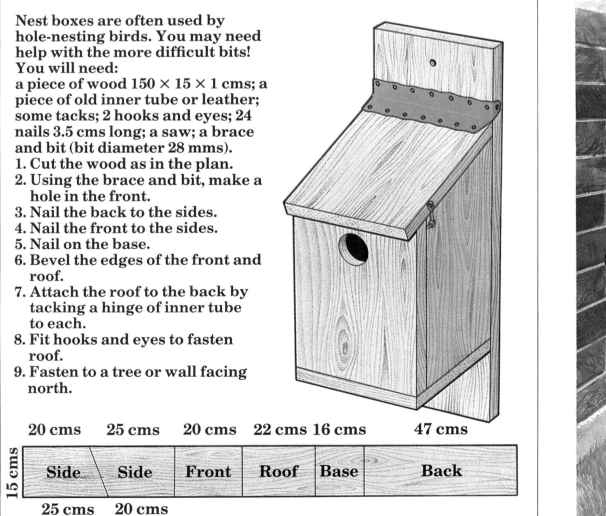

Blue tit

Song thrush

Blackbird

	20 cms	25 cms	20 cms	22 cms	16 cms	47 cms
15 cms	Side	Side	Front	Roof	Base	Back
	25 cms	20 cms				

A large garden will often become the summer home of a spotted flycatcher. They arrive from Africa in early May, and may be seen darting from a perch after a flying insect. Flycatchers usually build their neat nest-cup of cobwebs, moss and hairs on a ledge of a building, or against a tree-trunk. However, odd sites, such as this old kettle, are sometimes chosen.

A well-stocked bird table will attract many birds. Only put out food in winter, however. Many household scraps are suitable. These include cheese, bacon-rind, stale cake and baked potato skins. It is best to avoid large amounts of white bread. Never put out salted nuts or dessicated coconut. You will see many different birds.

Blue tit

Great tit

Song thrush

Lesser spotted woodpecker

Starlings

House sparrow

Greenfinch

Tree sparrow

Birds of the City

The centre of a busy city is a tightly-packed area of office-blocks, shops and churches. It is a noisy place, full of people, and often polluted by smoke and traffic fumes. It is unsuitable for most birds. There is little natural food apart from the insects that live on the occasional tree in streets and parks. Yet, a few species of bird have adapted to live in these surroundings. They have found that people can provide food, sometimes deliberately, but more often through waste. These birds have also found that ledges and holes in buildings are a good substitute for more natural nest-sites on cliffs or in trees. Town centres are also several degrees warmer than the countryside, especially in winter. The birds often have a better chance of survival in a crowded city during a cold winter.

The house sparrow has adapted well to town life. Large numbers nest in holes in roofs. They feed on spilled grain, scraps of bread and other waste. The black-headed gull is another familiar town bird, especially in winter. They are typical scavengers. They gather food on rubbish-dumps and playing fields and spend a good deal of time sitting on buildings or in park lakes. Late in the afternoon, they fly away from the city centre to roost on reservoirs or flooded gravel pits on the city's outskirts. As they leave, thousands of starlings fly into the city, on a winter's evening. They roost in warmth and safety among the buildings.

Perhaps the most typical bird-about-town is the feral or street pigeon. Pigeons live in crowded squares and other public places. They seem to enjoy the company of people, from whom they scrounge crusts and other food. Feral pigeons are the descendants of those which were once kept in large dovecotes as a source of fresh food.

Black redstarts are the most recent newcomers to city life. Several pairs were found breeding in London during the Second World War. They have since spread to other cities with derelict sites.

Swifts are summer visitors to towns and villages. They nest inside the roofs of buildings. On summer evenings, screaming parties of swifts hurtle round the roof-tops in their courtship chases. Swifts spend most of their lives in the air, catching flying insects and even sleeping on the wing.

Feral pigeons are popular with tourists, and the birds in London's Trafalgar Square are well aware of this! But pigeons are not **popular with everybody. Their droppings are unsightly and corrode statues and stonework. Pigeons are very comfortable in** **towns. There are holes and ledges for nesting, good food supplies, and fountains for drinking and bathing.**

This young kestrel hatched in a nest built on the ledge of a tall building, right in the middle of London. Kestrels hunt by hovering as they watch for small animals. In the country, they eat mice, voles and beetles. In town, house sparrows are their chief victims.

The black redstart is a rare bird. It has only come into towns in the last 50 years. It makes its home on derelict and industrial sites in the very hearts of some cities. Its nest will be tucked away among rubble or in a dark crevice in crumbling walls. It feeds mainly on spiders and insects such as greenfly which it finds easily in such places.

As dusk falls on a winter's evening, thousands of starlings fly in to roost in the city centre. It is warmer and probably safer here than in the surrounding countryside. In the morning, most of these birds fly out to the country or suburban gardens where they search for grubs, leatherjackets, worms and berries.

Farmland Birds

At any time of year, farmland is important for birds. Unfortunately, some of these birds are pests, raiding crops. Others help the farmer. They eat such harmful creatures as leatherjackets, wireworms and slugs. They also eat weed seeds. Today, birds that live in farming areas are having to cope with many changes. Fields have been made larger to make the best use of modern machinery. Thousands of kilometres of hedgerows have been removed. This not only destroys nest-sites, but also the insects, berries and seeds.

Other problems have been caused by the use of pesticides – chemicals which are sprayed on the land and crops to get rid of insects, weeds and fungal diseases. Some of these chemicals also poison birds – barn owls suffered particularly from the use of insecticides. Stubble burning is another hazard.

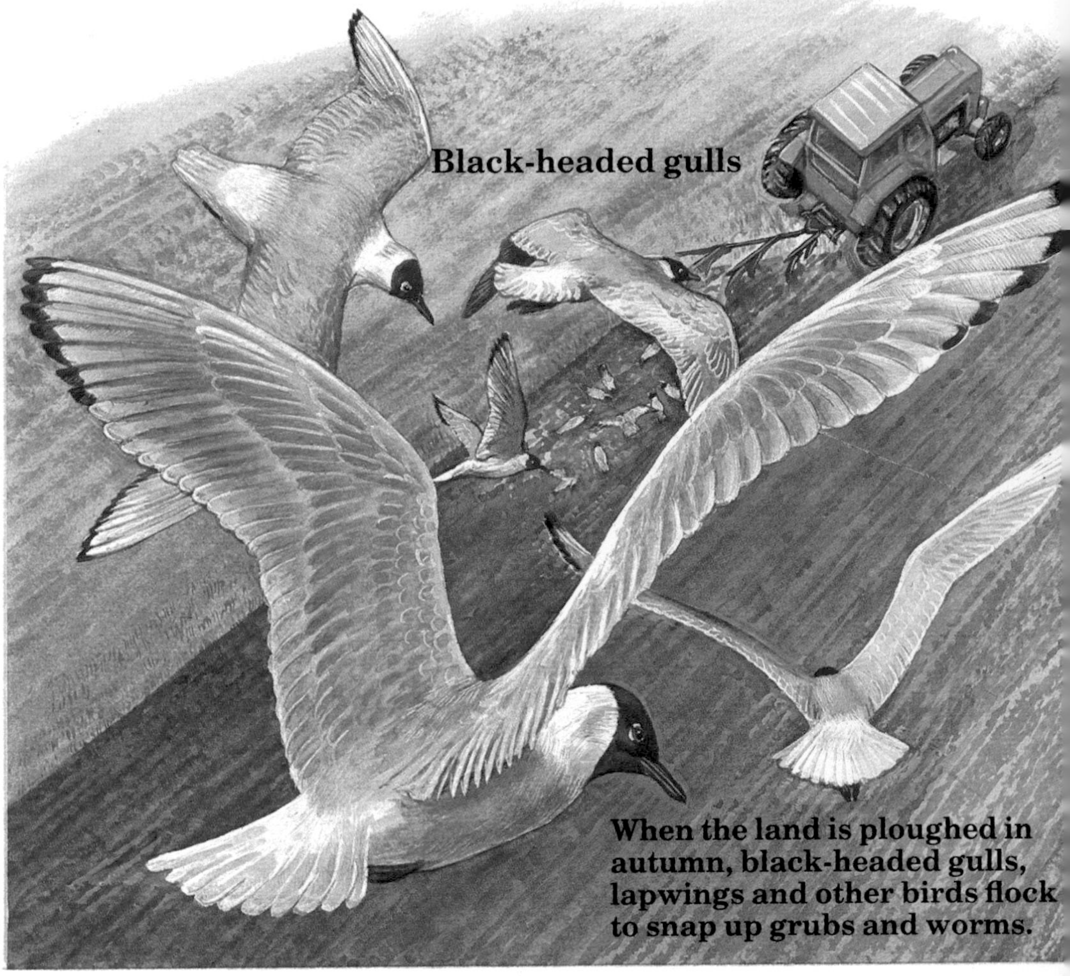

Black-headed gulls

When the land is ploughed in autumn, black-headed gulls, lapwings and other birds flock to snap up grubs and worms.

Pheasant

Grey partridge

Not all the birds of farmland nest in the hedgerows. In spring, lapwings are one of the first birds to establish their nesting territories. Watch out for their tumbling display-flights and listen for their noisy 'peewit' calls. Their nest is a shallow scrape in the soil, and their eggs are well camouflaged.

Rook

Wood pigeon

You can often see large flocks of woodpigeons and rooks on farmland, during the winter. Rooks help farmers by taking harmful grubs and wireworms. Woodpigeons, however, are a major pest. They eat newly planted grain and green crops.

Lapwings

Goldfinches

Tree sparrow

In late summer, the crops ripen and the grain is harvested. Large mixed flocks of finches and sparrows gather to roam the stubble fields and hedgerows. They are searching for spilled grain and ripe seed-heads.

Hedgerow Birds

Hedgerows have been part of the landscape for over a thousand years. A rich variety of plants and insects live in them, and they give homes to many small mammals and birds. The best hedges are usually the oldest, as they contain the greatest variety of bushes. You can judge the age of a hedge by counting the number of different kinds of shrub in a 30-metre stretch. Usually, there is one species for every hundred years. Hedges with trees and tall bushes provide nest-sites and song-posts for many woodland birds, including owls, woodpeckers and tits. Blackbirds, thrushes, warblers and finches nest in the thicker hedges. These also give ground-cover to pheasants, partridges, robins and buntings.

In the past, hedges were kept in good condition by the 'layering' method. Long stems were cut half-through at their bases and bent sideways. In spring, new growth added to the hedge's thickness. Sadly, the cheapest method of trimming a hedge today is by means of a slasher and tractor. This method cuts off unwanted growth but also destroys new saplings. The hedge loses both its thickness and its value to wildlife. In some parts of the country, hedges have been completely done away with and the landscape is bare and empty.

The cock yellowhammer's song, 'a-little-bit-of-bread-and-no-cheese', is well known. It sings from early spring to late summer. The hen builds a cup-shaped nest of grasses at

Thistles and teazles, blackberries and bryony are just some of the many seed and berry-bearing plants that grow in hedges. They are a rich store of food in autumn. Fieldfares, redwings and other thrushes are attracted by the bright colours and tasty flesh of the berries. Goldfinches enjoy thistledown. (Only adult goldfinches have the red face-patch.)

Bullfinch

Linnets have a tuneful, twittering song. They often nest in thick hedges, especially if there are gorse-bushes present, and waste-ground and weeds nearby. Both parents feed the young while they are in the nest. In winter, large flocks of linnets feed on the seeds of thistles and other weeds, or search for grain in stubble fields. In summer, they find insects in the hedgerows.

Whitethroats prefer the thickest hedges. The males often sing from a bush-top or in flight. They are insect-eaters and arrive in northern Europe from Africa in early spring. Their numbers have gone down in recent years.

he base of the hedge. Two broods are raised in most years. Yellowhammers have stout bills, well suited to seed-eating. In autumn they search the stubble for grain.

Goldfinches

Redwing

Fieldfares

Corn bunting

Woodland Birds

Forest covered most of northern Europe in prehistoric times. For many centuries, however, people have been at work, cutting it down to make way for fields and towns. Today there is little woodland left. The original forest was made up of broad-leaved trees such as oak, ash and beech. It often had a lower layer of hazel and other shrubs. Today we plant dense forests of pine, spruce and other quick-growing conifers. They are far less valuable to wildlife than the old broad-leaved woods with their greater variety of species.

The birds that live in woods have evolved special features to help them survive. They are often camouflaged in olive green and brown to match the leaves. They also have loud songs to communicate in their dense surroundings. Many woodland birds nest in natural holes. Woodpeckers have chisel-like bills for carving their own nest-holes. Their feet are special, too, with two toes forward, and two to the rear to grip the bark. Their tails have stiffened feathers for support.

The willow warbler has a liquid, descending song. It prefers woodland with a lower layer of shrubs. The closely related chiffchaff looks very similar. You can easily distinguish it from the willow warbler by its monotonous 'chiff-chaff' song.

The tiny wren has one of the loudest voices of any woodland bird. It needs a loud voice to establish a territory and attract a mate. The cock bird builds several nests each year. The female chooses one of them in which to lay her eggs. Wrens are very active, and search the tangled undergrowth for spiders and insects.

Trees have several ways of making sure that their seeds and nuts are well spread out. For example, jays feed heavily on acorns during the autumn. They often take them away and bury them as a store for the hard days of winter. Many of these stores are forgotten and the acorns eventually start to grow. Some oak forests may have spread by this means in the past. Jays also eat spiders and worms. They will even take the eggs and young of smaller birds. Listen for their ugly, raucous call.

The nightingale is one of our best known song-birds. Despite its name, it sings as much during the day as it does by night. It is difficult to see as it prefers the thickest parts of coppiced woodland and the dense shrub layer. It comes to Britain in the summer when insect life is at its most plentiful.

Woods are divided into several layers. Various species live in these layers. Some live all their lives at one level. Others use several, perhaps for different purposes. They may, for example, feed on the ground, nest among the shrubs, and sing in the canopy.

1. A mistle thrush sings from the tree-tops, and builds its nest in the fork of a tree.

2. A great spotted woodpecker carves a hole in a tree-trunk. In following years, the hole may be used by starlings, tits or nuthatches.

3. Nuthatches will cement up the entrance with mud, making it too small for starlings to enter.

4, 5, 6. Nightingales, wrens and robins sing and nest in the shrub layer. The robin also feeds on the ground and sings from high up in the trees.

7. The woodcock is perfectly adapted to life on the ground, with its 'dead-leaf' camouflage. Its long sensitive bill can probe for worms in the ground.

Nuthatches are found mainly in broad-leaved woodland. They are not common in the north. Nuthatches get their name from their habit of wedging nuts and seeds in cracks in the bark. Then they split them with heavy blows of the bill. Nuthatches can move head-first, up and down, clinging on with sharp claws.

31

Mountain and Moorland Birds

Conditions in the mountains are hard. The soil is infertile and weather conditions are severe. Few plants can survive here. As you go higher up the mountain, the trees that grow on the lower slopes disappear. They give way to heather, peat-bog and bare rock. This is partly due to the climate, but also to grazing by sheep which destroys tree seedlings. The creatures that live on high ground must be specially adapted to survive. Only a few stay all the year round. Some birds nest in the mountains but move as wintery conditions set in and food gets hard to find. Those that live here all the year round are rare, but often of great beauty. Even this remote habitat is threatened. There is increasing disturbance by visitors and walkers. Bogs are being drained, more land is being farmed, and vast areas are being planted with coniferous trees.

The ptarmigan is one of the few birds that live on high mountain-tops throughout the year. It changes its colour to escape predators. In winter, ptarmigan are pure white, matching the snow. In spring and autumn, they are 'half-and-half'.

Raven

Golden eagle

Dotterel

Red grouse

Some typical birds of high mountains, like the Cairngorms of Scotland, are shown here. In this habitat, many birds nest on the ground. These include red grouse, ptarmigan and the summer-visiting meadow pipits and dotterel. Others, like wheatears, nest in holes in the rocks and scree. These birds are superbly camouflaged to avoid being seen by golden eagles and buzzards. Predators like these will catch mountain hares, and eat carrion such as dead sheep. The raven is another well-known carrion-eater found in mountainous country.

n summer, their mottled brown
and grey blends perfectly with the
granite and lichen. The ptarmigan
is truly 'a bird for all seasons'.

Buzzard

Meadow pipit

Wheatear

Birds of Lakes

Any area of fresh water provides good opportunities to watch water-birds. People often feed ducks and swans on park lakes, so they become tame and easy to watch at close hand. Each species of water-bird is specially adapted to take its food from different depths in the water. Fishing birds, for example, like grebes and herons, have dagger-like bills for grabbing fish. Herons wade in the shallows. Grebes dive beneath the surface. There are two main groups of ducks: those that dabble to find food in the weed and mud of the shallows, and those that dive for underwater seeds and water insects. A third group, the fish-eating ducks, are seldom seen on small inland lakes. Swans and geese have long necks so they can make the best of both worlds. They both graze on grass, but they can also up-end to reach weeds.

'As bald as a coot' is a good description of the coot's white head shield. It thrusts it forward to frighten away other coots.

Coots are common on park lakes. They dive briefly for beakfuls of weed, which they then eat on the surface.

Little grebe

Mandarin ducks

As its name suggests, the Canada goose comes from North America. It was first introduced to northern Europe between two and three hundred years ago, in collections of ornamental birds. Some escaped and their descendants have become widespread. In spring the winter flocks split up to raise families.

Wherever fish are found, there is a good chance of seeing a grey heron. Herons will even come into small gardens to steal goldfish from a pond. They nest in large colonies called heronries.

Mute swan

Mallard duck

Tufted duck

Mallard ducks and mute swans are the most common birds on park lakes. Both dabble and up-end for food in shallow water. The mandarin duck is an ornamental species. Tufted ducks and little grebes dive beneath the surface using their legs as propellers. Tufted ducks catch swimming insects, while grebes are specialists at catching fish.

Birds of Rivers

The sources of rivers often occur high in the mountains. These areas receive large amounts of rain and snow during the year. Some of this water flows across the surface of rocks and soil, and collects in lakes and rivers. Finally it will flow away to the sea. Some water is soaked up by peat-bogs or porous rock. It disappears underground and only comes to the surface again as springs.

In its upper course, a mountain stream is a rushing torrent of water. The current is too swift to allow many plants to grow, but the water is clean and unpolluted. Because it is so turbulent, it dissolves much oxygen from the air. This is important because all animals that live in water need oxygen. These animals include the larvae of many insects. There are fish here, too — minnows and trout.

Of the birds that make their homes here, some are only summer visitors. The common sandpiper, for example, migrates south to warmer winter climates. Grey wagtails make for the lower course of the river. Even the dumpy dipper will abandon its favourite boulder and move downstream in harsh weather.

The character of the river changes as it approaches the lowlands. The river's flow is smoother and the valley sides are less steep. Towns and industries may be built along its banks. There is more chance of the water being polluted by human waste. But where the river meanders through lush water-meadows, its banks are lined by reeds and yellow flag iris. Coarse fish take the place of trout. Yellow wagtails snatch insects which have been flushed from the grass by grazing cattle. There is always a chance of catching a glimpse of the electric-blue streak of a kingfisher.

Above: The grey wagtail seldom lives far from rushing water. It has sulphur-yellow underparts, grey back, and black chin and tail. The female is more buff in colour.
Below: The yellow wagtail is smaller than its grey cousin, with an olive-brown back. It is a summer visitor and prefers the lower river valleys.

Kingfishers make their nest-holes in river banks. They use their bills as pickaxes and feet as shovels. An upward slope from the entrance keeps the water out. The eggs are laid on a pile of fish bones. By the time the young are big enough to leave the nest, it has become a very smelly place! By nesting in a hole, kingfishers are able to hide

The dipper lives beside fast-flowing mountain streams, with boulder-strewn beds. It is a remarkable bird because it can walk underwater! First, it jumps into the stream and faces into the current. Then it uses the force of the current to hold it down by making itself into a wedge-shape, arching its back and tail. Bubbles of air are trapped beneath the feathers and gleam like silver as it searches among the boulders and stones. It eats caddis, mayfly larvae and other food.

their bright colours. Otherwise they would be too easy for predators to spot. Kingfishers hunt by hovering and suddenly diving to catch small fish.

The goosander is a member of the duck family. It belongs to the group known as saw-bills, which have serrated inner edges to their beaks. These help the birds to grip the slippery fish on which they feed. The goosander is an efficient diver. It swims underwater by kicking with its legs as it chases its prey. It can stay underwater for a considerable time. It nests close to mountain rivers and lochs.

Birds of Reed Beds

Much of lowland Europe was once marshland and reed-beds. Ever since Roman times, however, and especially since the seventeenth century, man has drained them. The reclaimed land is now important for agriculture. In the past, reeds were harvested and used as thatch. There is much less demand for this today.

Reeds will only grow in still or gently flowing water. They do well at the edges of shallow lakes and meres. Gradually, they spread until a whole area which was once open water has become a reed-bed. Reeds are tall plants, often more than two metres. They provide good cover for a range of birds and other creatures. But as reed-beds have been drained, the animals are disappearing as well. Some have already become very rare indeed. One example is the bittern, a member of the heron family, superbly camouflaged to match dead reeds. It was common in East Anglia before the drainage of the Fens. By 1850 it had become extinct as a breeding species. Fortunately, with protection, it has returned to the Fens but there are still fewer than 40 breeding pairs in the whole of Britain. The bearded tit has also been seriously threatened. So has the marsh harrier, a spectacular reed-bed bird of prey.

These and other species will only survive if the few remaining areas of reed-bed are kept as wildlife reserves. A number of organizations try to protect wildlife in these areas. The RSPB runs successful reserves at Minsmere, Suffolk; Radipole, Dorset; and Leighton Moss in Lancashire.

The reed warbler is a common reed-bed bird. It is a summer visitor, feeding on moths, gnats, caterpillars and other marsh insects. The female weaves the neat, cup-shaped nest, which is carefully fastened to a few stiff reeds. Reed warblers seldom venture far into the open. They prefer to cling to the reeds, working from stem to stem as they search for food.

Bearded tits, sometimes called bearded reedlings, are only found in reed-beds, or very close to them. The male has a striking black moustache, while the female has a plain brown head. Bearded tits can be difficult to spot and are most often noticed by their 'pinging' call. Their stout bill is ideal for getting at insects and reed seeds. They build cup-shaped nests. Bearded tits suffer badly in very cold weather. This, coupled with the loss of reed-beds, has brought them to the verge of extinction in northern Europe on several occasions.

The water rail is more often heard than seen, as it lurks among the reeds. It only ventures into the open in the coldest weather. Then it stands motionless if disturbed, relying on camouflage for protection. It feeds on plants, worms, insects and even catches small fish.

The cuckoo is a brood parasite, which means it lays its eggs in the nests of other birds. Reed warblers are often the victims. The cuckoo's egg hatches more quickly than the others. Instinctively, the young cuckoo heaves other eggs or nestlings into a hollow in its back. It struggles, time and again, to the edge of the nest until it has pushed out all its rivals. It now has its foster parents' full attention. It grows so rapidly that it is soon too big for the nest.

39

Estuary Birds

The shallow water of an estuary is enriched by nutrients, washed down by the river. This is ideal for vast numbers of minute plants and animals called plankton. These organisms are food for many of the larger creatures that also live in the estuary – shellfish, worms, crustacea and fish. In their turn, these are the food of thousands of wading birds and wildfowl.

Shellfish are armour-plated. They can also tunnel into the mud. Sandhoppers and other crustacea hide among flotsam, and worms stay hidden in tunnels. Despite these defences, wading birds have evolved bills of different lengths to get at their food. Each species specializes at particular items. Only the oyster-catcher can chisel into a cockle or prize one open.

Twice a day, the tide covers the mud and sandbanks of the birds' feeding area. They fly off and make the most of this chance to roost.

In spite of their importance to wildlife, estuaries are often regarded as wasteland. Planners are only too keen to reclaim them for industry, farmland or airports. As a result, many have been spoiled or are seriously threatened.

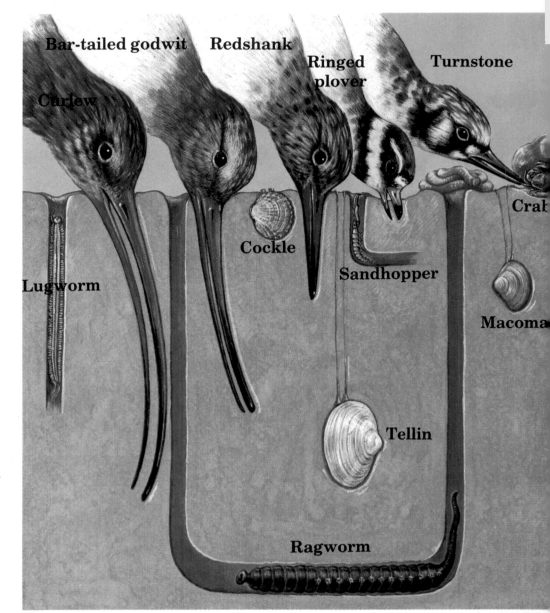

Estuary birds have long legs for wading and long bills for probing the mud. The long, sensitive bills of curlews and godwits can reach lugworms in their burrows.

Redshanks take the shrimp-like Corophium. Plovers have short bills and snatch food from the surface. Turnstones search the strand-line for food.

Many of the birds that visit Britain's estuaries come during the winter months. Others drop in during the autumn and spring to refuel while on migration. They are often en route between their Arctic breeding-grounds and their winter quarters which may lie south of the Equator. These sanderling will spend the winter on the sunny shores of southern Africa. Each year, British estuaries provide food for as many as 1½ million wading birds, at least half the European total.

From the middle of the 19th century, black-tailed godwits were extinct in Britain as a breeding species. But in 1952 they returned. They started breeding again on the water meadows of the Ouse Washes in East Anglia. Since then, they have been protected and their numbers have increased. In winter they fly to estuaries and are joined by others from Europe. They often form flocks of 50 or more. They feed by wading in water up to their bellies, probing in the mud for worms and shellfish.

Only a few greenshanks spend the winter in Britain. However they are not uncommon when passing through on their spring and autumn journeys. They use their long bills for probing and picking up food from the water. They will also chase shrimps and other small animals in pools and at the water's edge.

Redshanks are one of the most common estuary birds in winter. They often nest inland along damp river valleys in summer. Like other waders, they must feed while the tide is out and their feeding-grounds are exposed. They even feed during the hours of darkness. As the tide floods in, they fly to quiet areas above the high-tide mark. They should not be disturbed at this time, or they would have to use up precious energy and lose their sleep. They only rest when the tide is in.

Birds of Sea Cliffs

Seabirds spend most of their lives at sea, but they have to come to land to nest and raise their families. The shores of the British Isles are very important for seabirds. No fewer than 24 different species nest along them. Every year, Britain is home for as many as six million seabirds!

The more remote sea-cliffs of the north and west are specially important as 70 per cent of the world's razorbills breed there. There are also 16 gannet colonies in British waters, used by three-quarters of the world's gannets. Why should the British Isles be so important? The answers lie in its coastline, which is full of bays and cliffs. The coastal waters are shallow and warmed by the North Atlantic Drift current. This gives rise to a rich supply of food in the form of plankton and fish.

In spite of Britain's advantages, her seabirds face many threats. Oil spilled by tankers, North Sea oil developments and deliberate dumping of oil at sea kills thousands of birds. There are also problems of pollution by industry, a fall in food supply due to over-fishing, and increasing disturbance by holiday-makers.

Above: Lesser black-backed gul feed inland as well as at sea. Lik most gulls, they are scavengers and will take eggs and young of other birds. They nest on cliffs, shingle-banks and sand-dunes.

Below: The razorbill has short stubby wings. For this reason it likes to nest on cliff ledges with a sheer drop below, making it eas to take off. Razorbills prefer les crowded spots than the closely-related guillemots.

Bottom: Shags nest on exposed cliff ledges and boulders at the cliff's base. Their eggs are incubated on the adult's feet!

The puffin, like other members of the auk family, has decreased in numbers. This is mainly due to pollution at sea. It uses its large bill in its courtship displays. It can also use it to carry several fish at once. The fish are pushed against spikes inside the bill which give an excellent grip. In this way, it carries sand eels back to its young.

Kittiwakes are small gulls that spend most of their lives at sea. They eat all kinds of food, including plankton and small fish. Kittiwakes breed in large, noisy colonies, and often use narrow cliff ledges for their nests. In recent years, some have taken to nesting on buildings in ports and other coastal towns. They also nest on window ledges and other ledges on the sides of buildings.

lmost every part of a sea-cliff is
sed for nesting or feeding. If the
oil at the cliff-top is soft, it makes
possible home for hole-nesting
irds. The middle section will be
sed by several species if it has flat
r inward-sloping ledges so that
ggs cannot roll off. Other birds
est among the tumble of rocks at
e cliff base. Below the high-tide
ark, food such as seaweed and
hellfish is exposed.

Left: Puffins will nest in rabbit
burrows or dig holes of their own.
The female lays a single egg.

Below: Guillemots nest on broader
liff ledges. They lay pear-shaped
ggs that roll in a circle rather
han over the edge!

Above: As the kittiwake's nest
area is so small, the parent birds
cannot cough up food like other
gulls. The young must take food
from the back of their parents'
mouths.

Left: Purple sandpipers eat
shellfish, such as the periwinkle,
which they find at the cliff base.

Above: Fulmars look like gulls,
but in fact belong to a group
called 'tubenoses'. They are able
to glide great distances.

Index

Bar-tailed godwit 40
Bitterns 38
Blackbirds 13, 22, 28
Black redstarts 24–25
Buntings 28
Buzzards 18–19, 33

Camouflage 8–9
Chiffchaffs 30
Coots 34
Corn bunting 39
Cuckoos 12, 39
Curlews 40

Dippers 36–37
Dotterels 32–33
Ducks 6–7, 12, 34–35
Dunnocks 8, 22

Eagles 18, 32
Eggs 12–13, 17

Falcons 18
Feathers 6–7, 17
Feeding 12–13, 16, 18, 20–21,
  22, 40
Fieldfares 28–29
Finches 22, 27, 28–29
Flight 4–5
Fulmars 43

Gannets 5, 12, 42
Geese 10, 12, 14–15, 34–35
Godwits 40–41
Goldfinches 28–29
Goosanders 37
Grebes 12, 34–35
Greenfinches 23
Greenshanks 41
Grouse 8–9, 10, 32–33
Guillemots 12, 42–43

Gulls 24, 26, 42–43

Harriers 18
Hawks 18
Hearing 20
Herons 34, 35
House martins 13, 14

Jackdaws 12–13
Jays 17, 31

Keratin 6
Kestrels 19, 25
Kingfishers 7, 36–37
Kites 18
Kittiwakes 42

Lapwing 10, 26
Lesser whitethroat 15
Linnets 11, 28

Marsh harriers 38
Meadow pipits 32–33
Merlins 18–19
Migration 14–15
Moulting 6

Nests 12–13, 20–21, 22–23, 28,
  32, 42
Nightingales 31
Nightjars 8–9
Nuthatches 31

Ospreys 12, 18
Owls 4–5, 8, 16, 17, 18, 20, 26
Oyster-catchers 40

Partridges 26, 28
Pheasant 6–7, 8, 26, 28
Pigeons 7, 12, 24, 27
Plover 8–9, 40

Ptarmigan 8, 32–33
Puffins 12, 42

Ravens 32–33
Razorbills 42–43
Redshanks 40–41
Redwings 28–29
Reed warblers 38
Robins 8, 10–11, 12, 22, 28, 31
Rooks 12, 27

Sanderlings 40
Sandpipers 9, 36
Shags 43
Sight 18, 20–21
Snipe 10
Song 10–11
Sparrowhawks 17
Sparrows 7, 13, 22–23, 24, 27
Spotted flycatchers 22
Starlings 22, 25, 31
Swallows 5
Swans 4, 34–35
Swifts 24

Terns 12–13, 14
Thrushes 17, 22, 28–29, 31
Tits 12–13, 22–23, 31, 38
Turnstones 40

Wagtails 36
Warblers 15, 28, 30
Water rails 39
Wheatears 33
Whitethroats 29
Wings 4–5
Woodcocks 31
Woodpeckers 10, 12, 17, 22, 30
Wrens 13, 22, 30–31

Yellowhammers 28–29

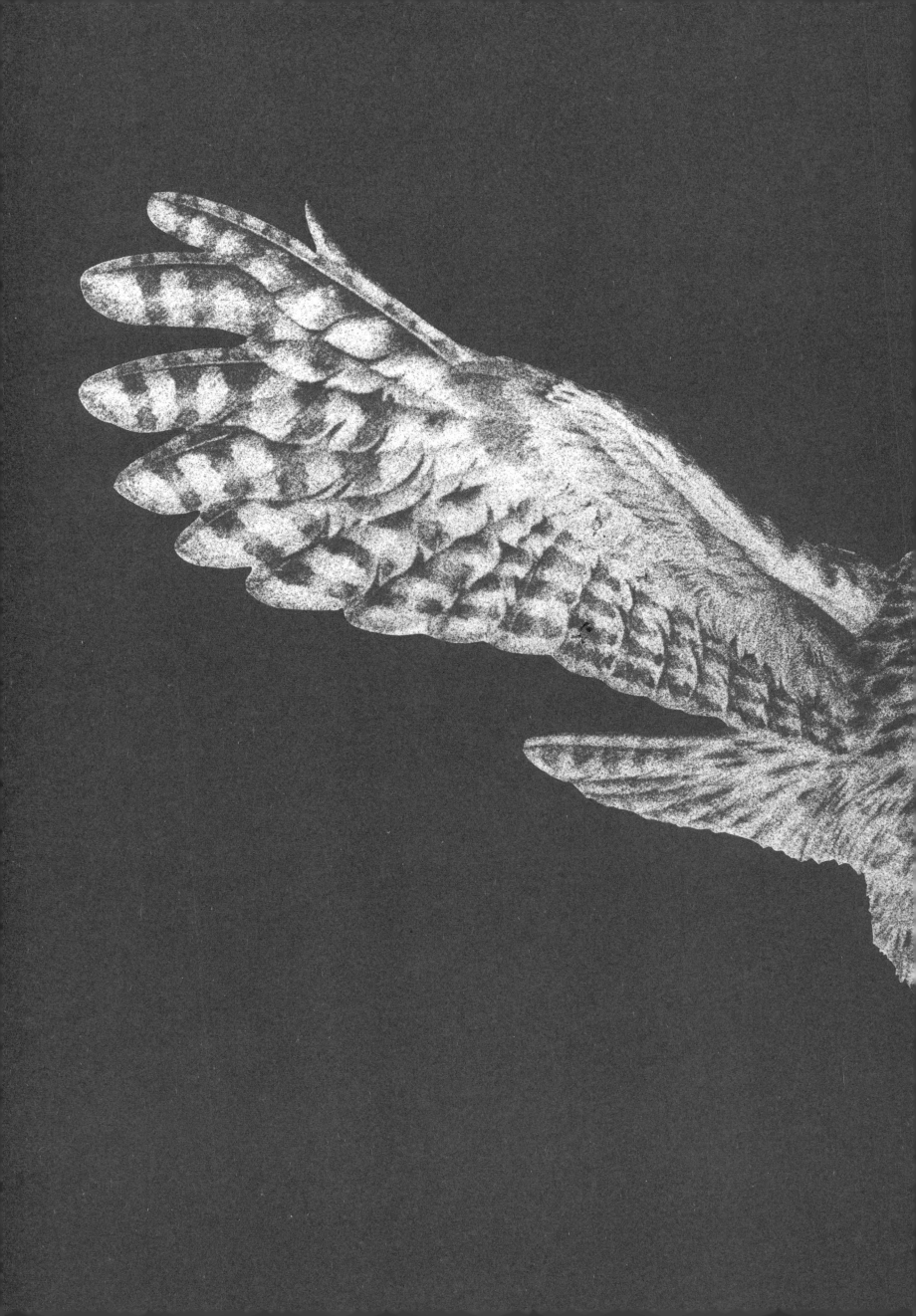